Richard Scarry's

Great Big Air Book

written
and
illustrated
by
Richard Scarry

RANDOM HOUSE · NEW YORK

This title was originally cataloged by the Library of Congress as follows:
Scarry, Richard. Richard Scarry's great big air book, written and illustrated by Richard Scarry. New York, Random House, [1971] 69 p.
col. illus. 33 cm. The animals learn how they depend on air to fly airplanes, dry laundry, blow out birthday candles, inflate tires, and
do many other things. [1. Air—Fiction. 2. Animals—Stories] I. Title. II. Title: Great big air book. PZ10.3.S287Rd [E] 77—146649
ISBN 0-394-82167-X 0-394-92167-4 (lib. bdg.)

A Spring Day

One spring morning a breeze blew
a feather in through the bedroom window.

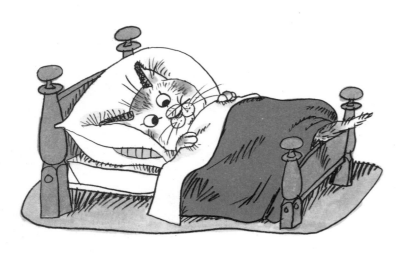

It tickled Huckle's nose.

"Aaah-chooo!" sneezed Huckle.

Huckle sneezed so hard that he
blew Little Sister out of bed.
"Oh, it must be windy today!" she said.

Huckle and Little Sister are
breathing in the fresh morning air.
Then they blow it out again.

You do it too. Breathe in! Breathe out!
When you blow out, you make the air move.
You make a little wind of your own.

After breakfast Miss Honey, the schoolteacher,
stopped by to take the children for a walk in the spring air.
A strong wind came in the door with her.

It was a very windy day.
The children felt the wind pushing against them.
   "Look at all the things the wind does,"
said Miss Honey. "It makes waves on the sea.
It makes the clouds move and the trees sway.
It even dries the clothes on the clothesline."

9

The air becomes warmer in springtime.
There is a sweet smell from the flowers,
and bugs fly back and forth through the air.
Flower seeds float on the spring breezes.
Colorful kites fly high in the sky.

narcissus

crocus

tulip

Lowly
Worm

daffodil

violet

lily of
the valley

Some people like to go for a drive
in the fresh spring air.

dandelion

Farmer Fox plows his field for spring planting.
The plow loosens the soil so air and water can get in.
The roots of the growing plants will need air and water.   11

"Oh, oh! It's going to rain," said Farmer Fox.
"My new tractor will get all wet.
Oops! I just felt a drop.
I must hurry for shelter!

"Hurry, Mother Cat!
Your laundry will get wet too.
Hurry everyone! We must help Mommy bring
the laundry into the house before it gets wet!"

13

Farmer Fox brought in Mommy's laundry
just in time. He brought in his tractor, too!
The laundry didn't get wet, and neither did his tractor.
    Everyone gathered around to have tea and cocoa
and cookies while waiting for the rain to stop.

In the kitchen Miss Honey had something else to show them.
"We all felt the big wind blowing outdoors today," she said.
"But right now, somewhere in this room, a *little* wind is blowing."
    She borrowed Lowly Worm's tiny hat, and placed it
over the spout of the boiling teakettle.
Hot, steaming air was coming out of the spout.
Suddenly it began to lift Lowly's hat up off the spout.
    "Hot air always rises," said Miss Honey.
"The hot, steaming air from the teakettle is making
a little wind right here in the kitchen.

"But don't worry, Lowly!
Your hat will come back down when the air cools off."

How Birds Fly

Birds can fly in the air.
Just watch Charlie Crow.
First, his legs push him
into the air.

Then his wings open. They move
upward and forward as he pulls
his legs close to his body.

GLUE

16

Then Charlie flaps his wings downward
and to the rear. His feathers close
tightly together again. The downward beat
of his wings moves him forward in the air.
He uses his tail feathers to steer.
    Now Charlie spreads his wings
to slow down. He is ready to land.

Oh, dear!
He stopped too fast!
He's a good flier,
but he doesn't always
land so well.

Harry Hyena thinks that if he glues
feathers on his arms and tail—and then
flaps his arms—he will be able to fly
like a bird.
    Well, he is wrong.

Mother's Busy Day

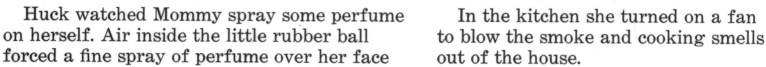

Huck watched Mommy spray some perfume on herself. Air inside the little rubber ball forced a fine spray of perfume over her face and hair.

In the kitchen she turned on a fan to blow the smoke and cooking smells out of the house.

Then she used a vacuum cleaner to suck up dust and dirt from the floor.

Little Sister had nothing to do, so Mommy blew up her wading pool. It took a lot of air.

Huckle wasn't bothering Mommy. He was kicking his ball. The ball was hard and firm because it was full of air.

Ha! Ha! you missed!

18

Some flies got into the house. Mommy chased them with a can of insect spray. Air in the can forced out the spray.

Then Mommy washed some clothes. Hot air
in the clothes drier dried the clean laundry.

She baked a pie and left it on the
window sill for the breeze to cool.

While she was driving to town, Mommy
noticed that one tire was soft. She blew
it up again with an air pump. Not too much
air now, Mamma!

At the hairdresser she sat
under the hair drier. The warm air
dried her freshly washed hair.

Back home again, Mommy started supper.
But when she tried to light the oven,
a strong breeze blew out the match.
Then another. And another!

After a while she said, "I just wish
that breeze would stop blowing."
"But, Mommy," said Huckle, "if air
didn't move and blow around, you
couldn't have done all the things you
did today."
"I guess you are right," she said.
And with her very next match she was able
to light the oven.

A Summer Picnic

It was a bright, sunny summer day.
There was not a cloud in the sky.
Miss Honey and her boyfriend, Bruno,
decided to take all the children on a picnic.

They drove past a lake where
some fishermen were fishing.
Oh, oh! They seem to have caught something!

While they were setting out the picnic,
Rudolf Strudel, the famous airplane pilot,
dropped by.

"Miss Honey!" he said. "A big thunderstorm
is coming this way. You and the children must
take shelter immediately!"

Ants always
come to picnics!

21

Everyone had been too busy putting out food to notice
the black storm clouds gathering in the sky.
"Hurry!" Rudolf warned. "The rain will start any minute."

C-r-a-a-a-a-c-c-k-k-k!
The lightning flashed! The thunder roared!
But everyone was safely inside the school bus.

22

No one got even the tiniest bit wet.
Not even Farmer Fox's tractor.
It was the best rainy-day picnic ever.

How Airplanes Fly

control tower

Father Cat took Huckle and
Little Sister to the airport
to meet Rudolf, the famous pilot.
He was going to show them how to fly
an airplane.

First, Rudolf pointed to the cockpit.
"The pilot sits here," he said. "He
flies the airplane with the stick, the throttle,
and the pedals. The stick is used to move
the elevators on the rear wings up and down.
They help the plane to fly lower or higher.

"The stick also moves the ailerons on the
front wings up and down. These help to make
the plane tip sideways and turn. The pedals
move the rudder on the tail. This helps
the plane to turn smoothly.

rudder

tail

cockpit

elevator

propeller

fuselage

nose

aileron

wing

landing
gear

a mechanic
fixing a motor

"The spinning propeller pulls the plane forward,
and makes air slip around the wing. The air that
goes over the curved top of the wing moves fast.
But along the straight bottom of the wing the air moves slower.
This makes it push harder, and it lifts the plane up, up
into the sky."

"One day I'll fly an airplane,"
said Huckle.
"Yes, maybe," said Rudolf.
"But for now come flying
with me."

Huck Takes Flying Lessons

"First, everyone fasten his seatbelt," said Rudolf.
"I will start the engine and set the propeller to spinning.
Down the runway we speed. Faster! Faster!

A Fall Through the Air

"With the stick, I can also
make the plane tip sideways
by moving the ailerons on the wings
like this....The plane leans
over sideways.

"I push the stick forward.
The elevators are pulled down.
This forces the nose of the plane down.

"I pull back on the stick
and level out.

"I pull back on the stick.
The elevators are pulled up.
The moving air strikes them and pushes
the tail down. This, together with the
pressure under the wings, forces the nose up.
I fold up the landing gear and push
the stick forward a little bit.
Now we are flying level."

"Now I climb steeply.

"Then I turn over.
I...!

"Oh! Oh! I've fallen out!
I forgot to fasten
my seat belt.

"But I, Rudolf Strudel, am lucky!
I never fail to wear my parachute.
The air is trapped in the parachute,
letting me fall slowly to earth.
But I wonder if Huckle will be able to land
the plane safely all by himself."

27

Huck Lands the Plane

Huckle quickly grabbed the control stick and located the pedals.

By working the rudder, the ailerons, and the elevators just as Rudolf had shown him, he started to come down and land.

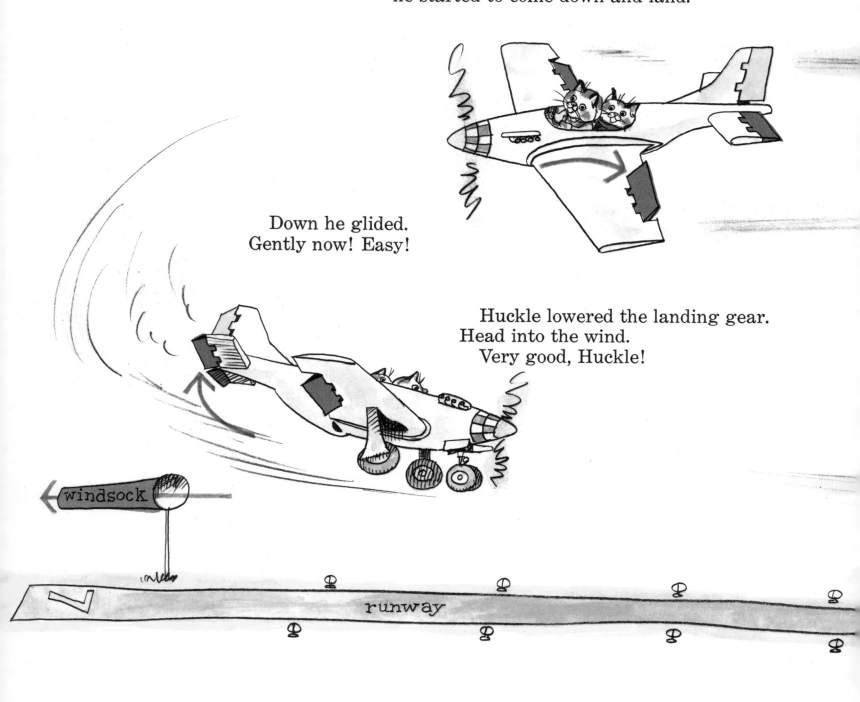

Down he glided.
Gently now! Easy!

Huckle lowered the landing gear.
Head into the wind.
Very good, Huckle!

windsock

runway

TOUCHDOWN! A perfect landing.
You are an excellent pilot, Huckle.

. . . and another perfect landing.
Right in the pickle barrel!
Very good, Rudolf.

A Rescue by Air

flag

bath house

1 2 3

In the summer the air is hot. It is fun to go to the beach and enjoy the cool ocean breezes. Mathilda could hardly wait to put on her new rubber tube and go for a swim. She was sure that the air in the tube would keep her from sinking.

beach umbrella

tent

doll

shovel

pail

sand castle

starfish

balloon

DRINK WATER

blimp

EAT BRUNO'S HOT DOGS

BRUNO'S HOT DOGS

LIFE GUARD

life guard

paper plates

Al, the lifeguard, sat on his stand, watching the swimmers. It was his job to rescue any swimmers in trouble.

seashell

sand flea

ball

crab

surfer

waves

a diving pig

lobster

Suddenly Al heard someone shouting, "HELP!"

He jumped down from his stand and rushed into the huge waves.

It was Mathilda.
The wind had carried her too far from shore.
She couldn't swim back.

But Mathilda was much too big for Al to save all by himself.
Not only that!
Now *he* was in trouble too.
Who could rescue *him?*

What good luck! Just in time
the Coast Guard helicopter came
to the rescue. It picked Al and
Mathilda up out of the sea.

The helicopter flew them safely back
to the beach, where Huckle unhooked them.
Mathilda promised Al that she would be
more careful the next time she went
swimming on a windy day.

At the Air Fair

There is a fair at the airport.
Everyone has come to see, or take rides in,
the old-fashioned airplanes. All these
old airplanes have propellers to help them
fly through the air.

Attention, all pilots!
Please do not bump into
any runaway balloons.

Spirit of St. Louis

There is a new jet airplane at the fair, too.
Jet planes don't need propellers to make them fly.

Look at Benny Baboon. He is going to show you
something with a toy balloon.

First, he blows up the balloon with air.
But he does not tie a knot in it.
Instead, he lets go of the balloon.
The air begins to rush out of the hole
at the end. As the air rushes out,
it pushes the balloon away from Benny.

control tower

weatherman

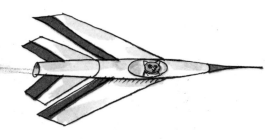

The air is going . . .

going . . .

gone!

Rudolf's jet plane engine works
a little like a balloon.
Up front, air is sucked into the engine.

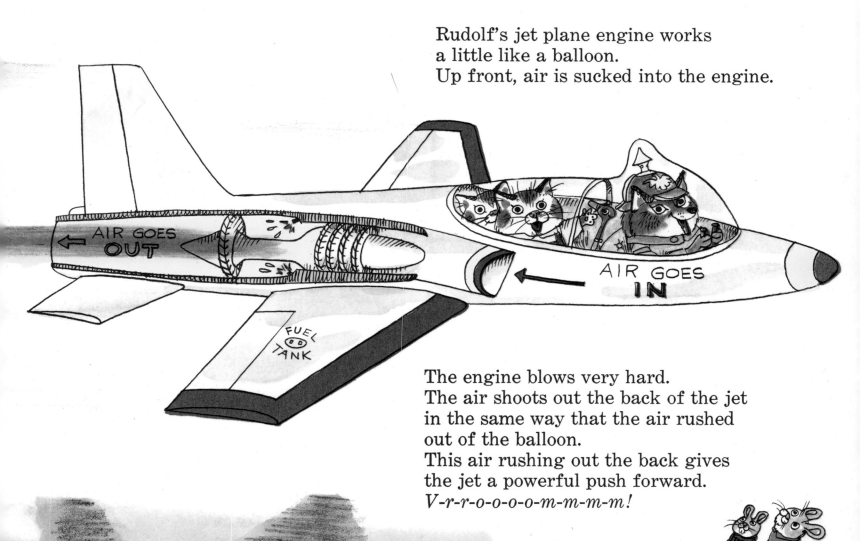

AIR GOES OUT

FUEL TANK

AIR GOES IN

The engine blows very hard.
The air shoots out the back of the jet
in the same way that the air rushed
out of the balloon.
This air rushing out the back gives
the jet a powerful push forward.
V-r-r-o-o-o-o-m-m-m-m!

Air Pollution

Doesn't Father Cat look nice
in his new, clean white suit?
He is going out for a walk
in the fresh air.
He is smoking a big, black cigar.
Don't get your clean white suit
dirty, Father Cat!

Father Cat walked down the street,
waving to all his friends.

He saw Janitor Joe mowing the school lawn.

He stopped to watch a power shovel
dig a big hole in the ground.
He saw a truck fall into that hole.

Down at the waterfront, where the city garbage
was being burned, he watched some fishermen.

Then he walked to the beach, where he ate lunch at Bruno's hot dog stand. Everyone likes to eat hot dogs at the beach.

Can you tell which little pig has already finished his hot dog?

Father Cat stopped at the railroad station. There he bought a bigger black cigar. He had to wait for a train to pass.

"That's a nice gray suit you are wearing," called Casey, the engineer.

Father Cat was almost home when
Rudolf swooped down to wave hello.

As soon as Father Cat got home,
he looked at himself in the mirror.

"My new white suit!" he cried.
"It's filthy! Why don't they do
something about that dirty, polluted air?"

"But you were making smoke too with your cigar," said
Mother Cat. "None of us should burn things any more than
we have to . . . if we want to keep our air fresh and clean."

That's right, Mommy.
But what's all that smoke
coming out of your kitchen?
Are *you* burning something?

Grandma's Birthday Party

The Cat family was going to visit Grandma on her birthday.
They rode in a taxi to the small country airport nearby.

There they climbed into a helicopter to go
to the big city airport.

On the way they saw Sergeant Murphy down below.
He was unscrambling a big traffic jam. Everyone
seemed to be heading toward the airport.

At the city airport, the whirling blades gently lowered
the helicopter to the ground. For the rest of the journey
the Cat family would travel by jet airliner.

43

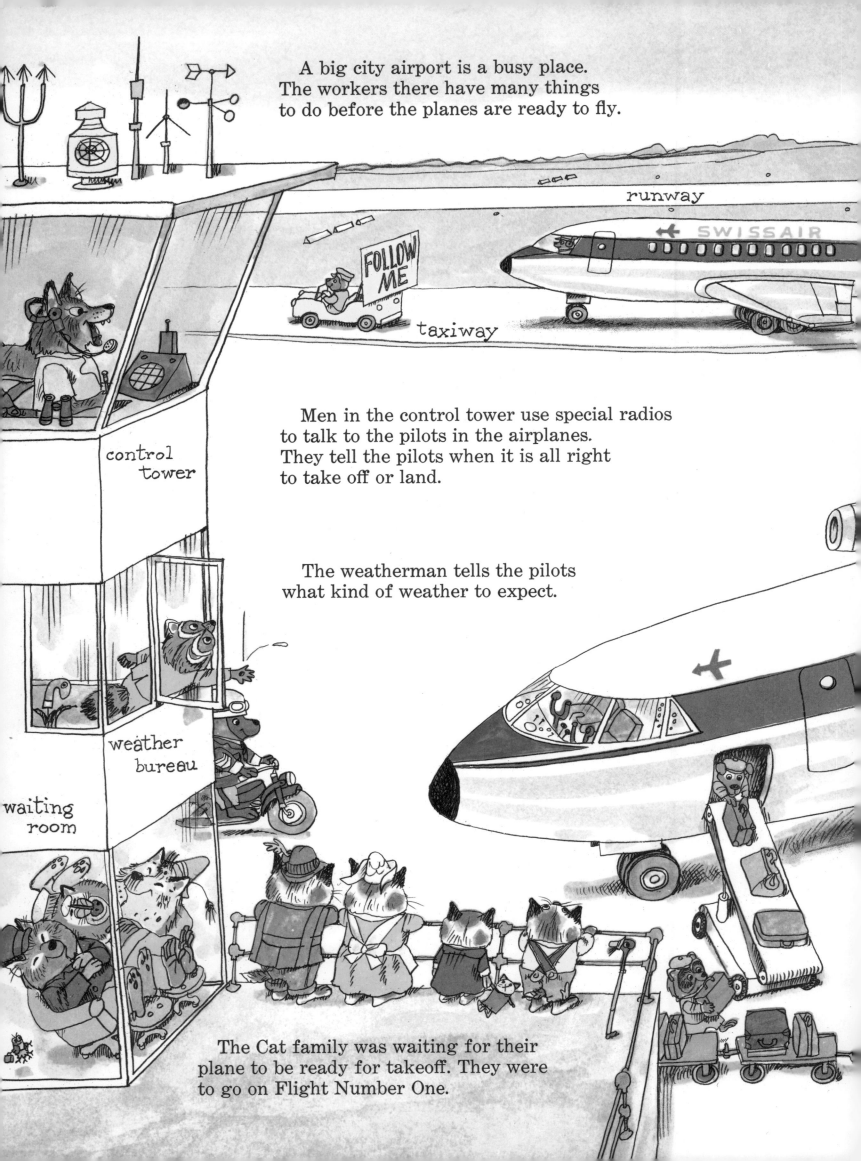

A big city airport is a busy place.
The workers there have many things
to do before the planes are ready to fly.

runway

FOLLOW ME

taxiway

SWISSAIR

Men in the control tower use special radios
to talk to the pilots in the airplanes.
They tell the pilots when it is all right
to take off or land.

control tower

The weatherman tells the pilots
what kind of weather to expect.

weather bureau

waiting room

The Cat family was waiting for their
plane to be ready for takeoff. They were
to go on Flight Number One.

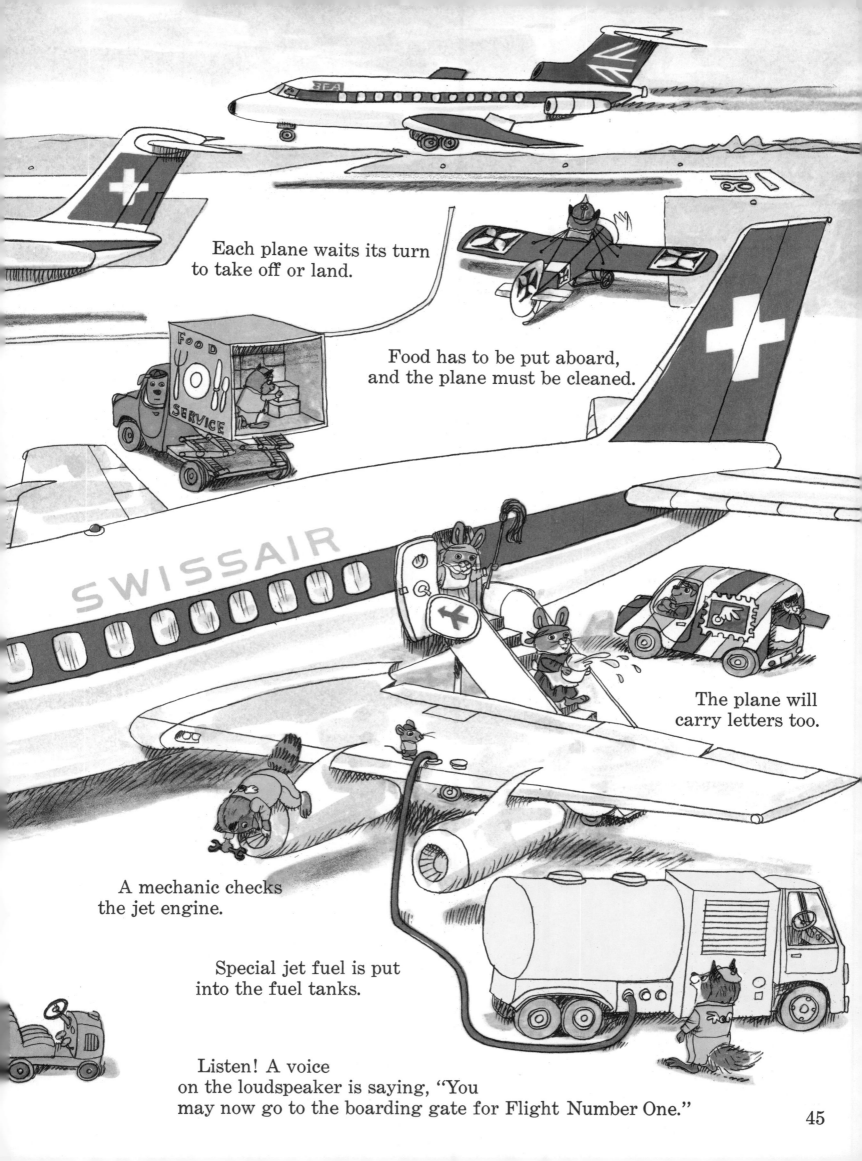

Each plane waits its turn
to take off or land.

Food has to be put aboard,
and the plane must be cleaned.

The plane will
carry letters too.

A mechanic checks
the jet engine.

Special jet fuel is put
into the fuel tanks.

Listen! A voice
on the loudspeaker is saying, "You
may now go to the boarding gate for Flight Number One."

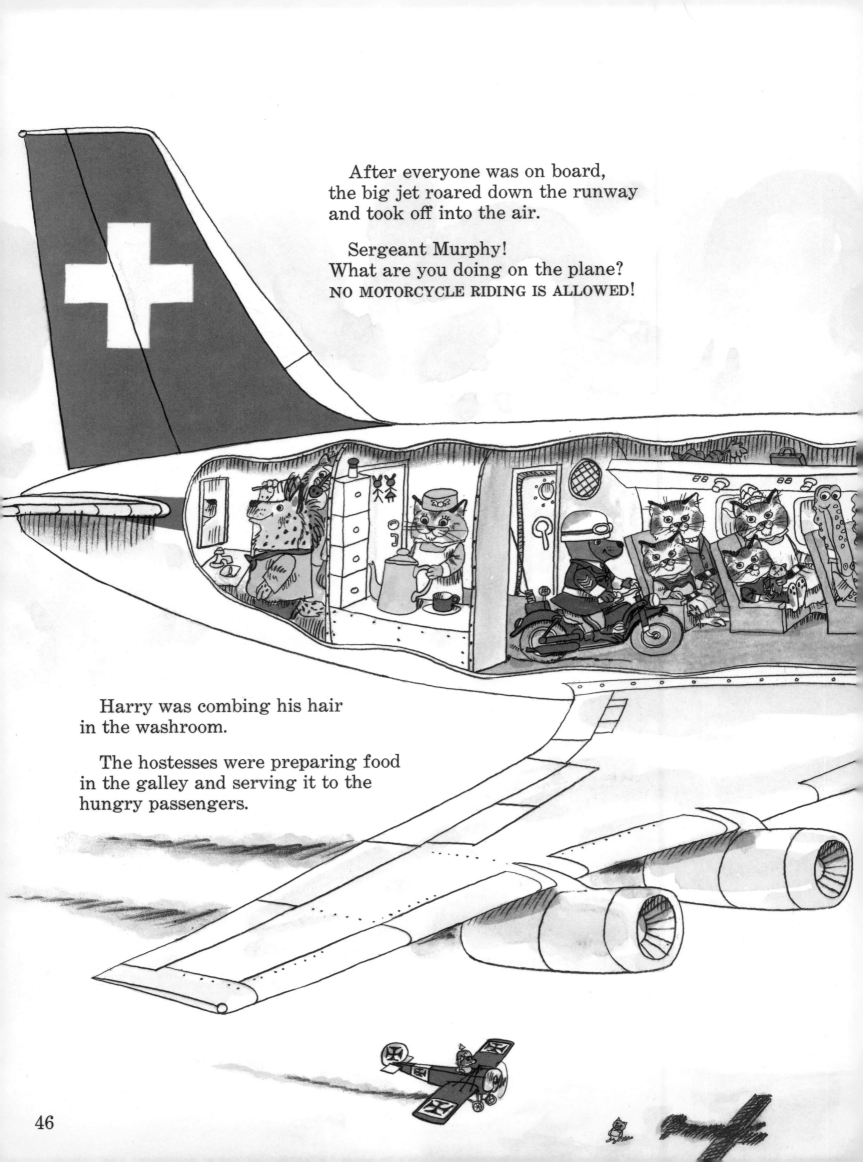

After everyone was on board,
the big jet roared down the runway
and took off into the air.

Sergeant Murphy!
What are you doing on the plane?
NO MOTORCYCLE RIDING IS ALLOWED!

Harry was combing his hair
in the washroom.

The hostesses were preparing food
in the galley and serving it to the
hungry passengers.

Every plane flies in the air lane assigned to it.
In that way, planes don't bump into each other.

Captain Fox is flying the plane
with the help of his co-pilot.
The navigator is planning the plane's
route in the sky.

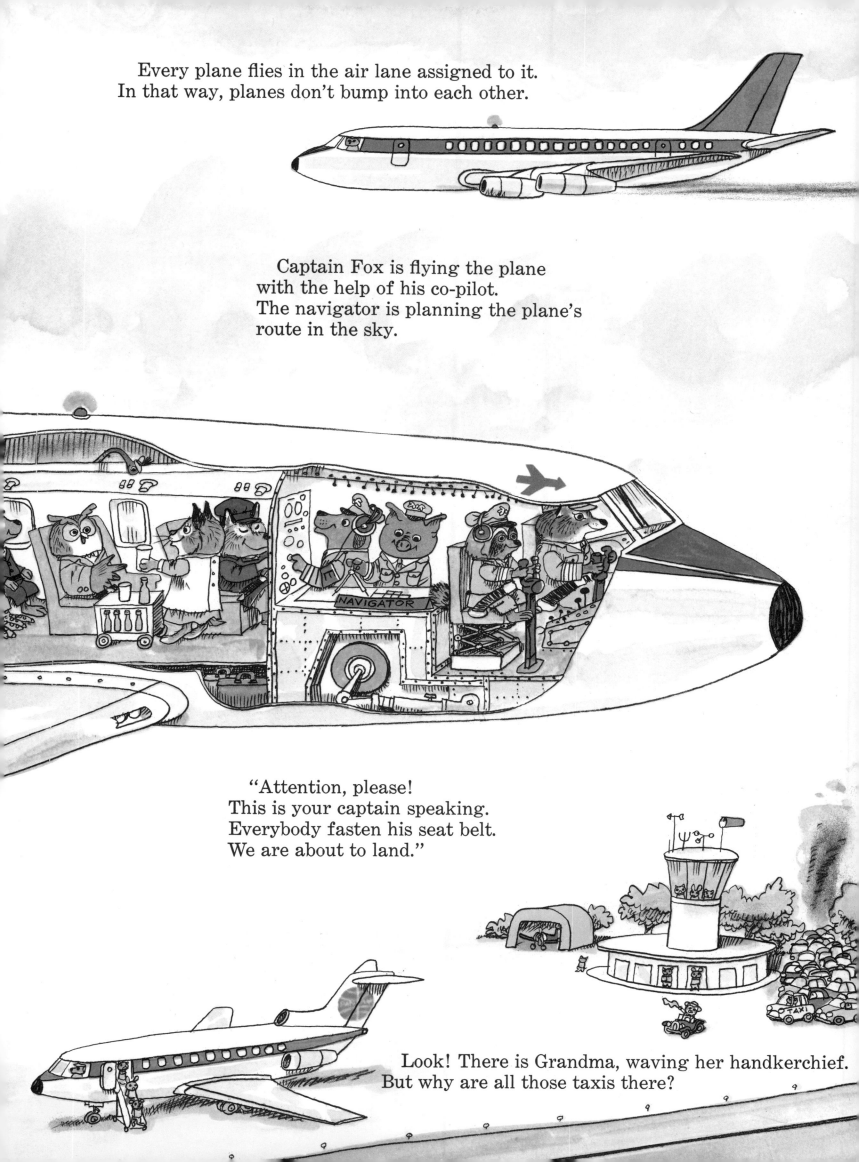

"Attention, please!
This is your captain speaking.
Everybody fasten his seat belt.
We are about to land."

Look! There is Grandma, waving her handkerchief.
But why are all those taxis there?

The Cat family's plane landed,
and Lowly gave Grandma a big kiss.
A lot of other planes landed, too.
Everyone was coming to Grandma's birthday party.
That was why Grandma had brought along so many taxis.
They were going to take all her friends to her house.

Sergeant Murphy had come along
just to unscramble the big taxi jam!
A good thing, too, or no one would ever get to the party.

"Why, Rudolf!" shouted Sergeant Murphy.
"How did you ever get your plane into this traffic jam?"

Air is *very* important
for blowing out birthday candles.
Grandma's cake had so many candles
she couldn't blow them out all by herself.
So all her friends helped her.
W-H-O-O-O-O-S-H!
Happy birthday, Grandma!

Grandma had such a good time at her party
that she can hardly wait until next year.

51

An Autumn Fire

In the autumn the leaves fall from the trees.
The smell of burning leaves is in the air.
Farmer Fox and his family and friends must
gather the crops before the cold winter comes.

Philip is carrying grain to the mill.
The wind makes the windmill spin.
Inside the mill, the grain is ground into flour.
Bread will be made with the flour.

OLD FARMER FOX'S ROADSIDE STAND

nuts

taffy apples

jelly

APPLES

apple cider

Farmer Fox is picking juicy red apples.

Mother Fox sells the harvest foods at her roadside stand.
Just a minute! Look there!
Do you see what Huckle sees?

A FIRE!!!
It has reached Farmer Fox's ladder.
Hurry, Mrs. Fox! Call the firemen.

OLD FARMER FOX'S
ROADSIDE STAND

APPLES

WATER
17

Before Mother Fox can hang up the phone,
the firemen come racing to the rescue.

Smokey, the fireman, turns on
the water too soon. The hose wiggles
and squirms out of control, squirting
water everywhere.

WATER
17

54

The force of the water is knocking apples
and apple pickers out of the trees.
Someone, please grab that hose!

Huckle finally gets hold of it
and puts out the fire. He has saved
Farmer Fox's roadside stand from burning down.
Water can put out fires because it keeps
air away from them. Fires can't burn
without air.

Farmer Fox gives everyone
a taffy apple to celebrate.
Mmmm! Taffy apples taste delicious
in the crisp autumn air.

Orchestra Practice

When Huckle beats his drum,
the top of it shakes back and forth
very fast. This makes a loud noise.
The sound speeds through the air.
Mother Cat hears it with her ears.

The door opens and in walks
Miss Honey with the class orchestra.
They are all going to practice
at Huckle's house today.

What in the world has Miss
Honey got in that huge case?

At last everyone has his instrument
unpacked and ready to play.

"Get set! Play!" says Miss Honey,
and the music begins.

cymbals

violin

bass drum

Miss Honey
plays the
bass fiddle

harp

accordion

guitar

bassoon

tuba

saxophone

trumpet

clarinet

Some instruments are played by blowing into them.
The air inside moves back and forth very fast.
This makes the sound your ears hear.

flute

trombone

But Huckle beats on his drum with his drumsticks,
while Lowly sings very loudly.
"Ow-wa-e-e-a-a-h-h-a-," goes Lowly's voice.

The sounds that Huckle and his friends make
travel through the air. Their music is so loud
that it shakes Mother Cat and Little Sister
right out of their chairs.

Huckle and the class orchestra certainly know
how to make themselves heard, don't they?

A Snowstorm

In wintertime the air is very cold.
Instead of rain, there is often snow.
The strong winds howl and blow.
Sometimes the snow falls and falls,
getting deeper and deeper.
This kind of snowstorm is called a blizzard.
Blizzards can cause a lot of trouble.

The firemen were trying to get to Ma Pig's
to put out a fire in her kitchen.
But a snowplow had to plow a path for them.
Would they get there in time?

Pa Pig was riding home from work in the train.
But tonight it was stuck in a snow drift.
Would he have to spend the night there?

The wind and snow and ice had
knocked down the electric wires.
Many houses had no light.
Others had no heat.

The delivery man and the school bus
were both stuck in the snow.

Doctor Dog was tramping
through the snow on snowshoes.
He was trying to visit
a sick patient.
"Will this snow never
stop falling?" he asked.

At last the snow *did* stop falling.
The blizzard ended. Pa Pig finally got home from work.
The firemen put out the fire in time.
Doctor Dog saw his sick patient.
But the school bus and the deliveryman
were still stuck in the drifts.
    "No school today!" said Miss Honey.
Instead, everyone had fun playing
out in the snow.

saucer

bobsled

sled

skis

ski

Be careful,
Miss Honey!

snowball

snowfort

Just look at all the things you can do
in the clear, cold, winter air.

chalet

snowshoes

snow cat

snowman

You can even make
a tiny cloud with your breath.

hockey stick

ice rink

ice skater

61

A Trip to the Moon

Wolfgang Wolf, Benny Baboon, and Harry Hyena
are about to climb aboard their spacecraft.
They are going to the moon to collect rock
samples and bring them back to earth.
They want to find out what the moon is made of.

Ready for lift-off.
Five, four, three, two, one, LIFT-OFF!
Up, up goes the spacecraft—
off into space and heading for the moon.

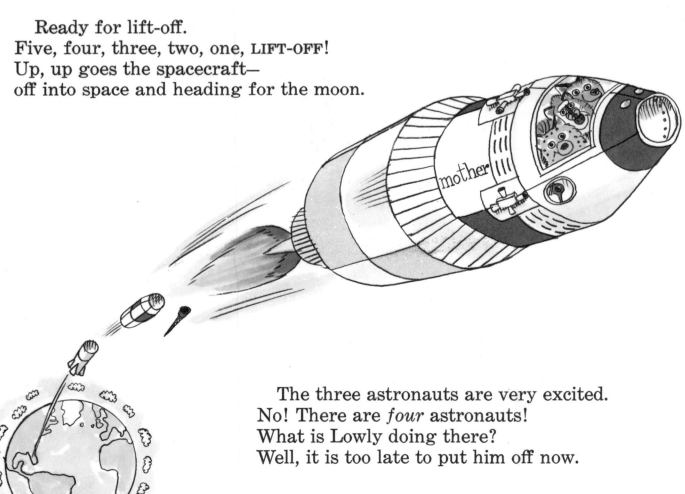

The three astronauts are very excited.
No! There are *four* astronauts!
What is Lowly doing there?
Well, it is too late to put him off now.

The spacecraft is getting close to the moon.
The landing ship (*Baby*) is attached
to the command ship (*Mother*).
Wolfgang turns the nose of the command ship
around so that it fits into the hatch door
of the landing ship.

Then Benny, Harry and Lowly climb
through the hatch door into the landing ship.
Wolfgang stays behind in the command ship
to wait for their return.

The two ships separate so that the landing
ship can head for the moon.

Benny! Turn on your landing motor
so you can make a gentle landing on the moon.

The ship trips over a rock.
It does not land very gently.

There is no air on the moon.
Each astronaut has to carry his air
with him. It is carried in a tank
in the pack on the astronaut's back.
    But Lowly has no space suit
so he gets into Harry's suit.
Now he too can breathe air.
    Pick, pick, pick.
They are busy collecting rock samples.

It is time to climb back into the landing ship.
The air in the astronauts' tanks is almost all used up.
Inside the landing ship there is plenty of air for breathing.

Oh, dear!
The hatch door
won't stay closed!

The air inside the landing ship will leak out.
"Keep calm," says Lowly. "Benny, you hold the door shut.
Harry, you turn on the air tank. Then I will be able
to breathe when I get out of your spacesuit. *I* know
how to keep that hatch door closed."

Lowly ties himself in a knot
around the door handle, and the door
stays tightly shut.
"Now we will be able to get back
with our valuable rocks," says Lowly.

All set?
BLAST-OFF!
The landing ship takes off from the moon,
leaving its launching pad behind.

It connects with the command ship again.
Then the astronauts climb through the nose hatch
into the other ship.

As soon as they are all set,
Wolfgang sends the empty landing craft
into space. Then the command ship
heads back to earth.

After the astronauts get back into the earth's atmosphere
they open up the big parachutes on their spaceship.
An aircraft carrier and several helicopters are waiting
to pick them up out of the sea.
HERE THEY COME! ...

But the spaceship does not land in the water.
It goes ... RIGHT DOWN THE SMOKESTACK!
Well, anyhow the astronauts have landed
safely with their precious rocks.

Everyone is happy to see
the brave astronauts safely back on earth.

After they have all had a bath,
the admiral gives Lowly a shiny medal.
On the medal are the words:

*"Lowly Worm, a real astro-knot.
The first worm on the moon."*

Lowly likes his medal very much.
But best of all he likes being back on earth
where he can breathe fresh air again.
All right, everyone! Let's all take
a deep breath of the earth's wonderful air!

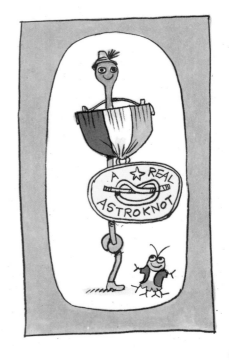